DEAR SPECIMEN

THE NATIONAL POETRY SERIES

The National Poetry Series was founded in 1978 to ensure
the publication of five poetry books annually through five
participating publishers. Publication is funded annually
by the Lannan Foundation, Amazon Literary Partnership,
Barnes & Noble, the Poetry Foundation, the PG Family
Foundation and the Betsy Community Fund, Joan Bingham,
Mariana Cook, Stephen Graham, Juliet Lea Hillman Simonds,
William Kistler, Jeffrey Ravetch, Laura Baudo Sillerman,
and Margaret Thornton. For a complete listing of generous
contributors to the National Poetry Series, please visit
www.nationalpoetryseries.org.

2020 COMPETITION WINNERS

Dear Specimen by W. J. Herbert
Chosen by Kwame Dawes for Beacon Press

[WHITE] by Trevor Ketner
Chosen by Forrest Gander for University of Georgia Press

Borderline Fortune by Teresa K. Miller
Chosen by Carol Muske-Dukes for Penguin Books

Requeening by Amanda Moore
Chosen by Ocean Vuong for Ecco

Philomath by Devon Walker-Figueroa
Chosen by Sally Keith for Milkweed Editions

DEAR SPECIMEN

SPECIMEN

POEMS

W. J. HERBERT

Beacon Press
Boston

Beacon Press
Boston, Massachusetts
www.beacon.org

Beacon Press books
are published under the auspices of
the Unitarian Universalist Association of Congregations.

24 23 22 21   8 7 6 5 4 3 2 1

This book is printed on acid-free paper that meets the uncoated
paper ANSI/NISO specifications for permanence as revised in 1992.

Text design by Nancy Koerner at
Wilsted & Taylor Publishing Services

Library of Congress Cataloging-in-Publication Data

Names: Herbert, W. J., author.
Title: Dear specimen : poems / W. J. Herbert.
Description: Boston : Beacon Press, [2021] | Series: The national poetry
    series
Identifiers: LCCN 2021016073 (print) | LCCN 2021016074 (ebook) | ISBN
    9780807007594 (trade paperback ; acid-free paper) | ISBN 9780807007600
    (ebook)
Subjects: LCGFT: Poetry.
Classification: LCC PS3608.E7325 D43 2021 (print) | LCC PS3608.E7325
    (ebook) | DDC 811/.6—dc23
LC record available at https://lccn.loc.gov/2021016073
LC ebook record available at https://lccn.loc.gov/2021016074

CONTENTS

~ V ~

FOREWORD

At the end of her collection *Dear Specimen*, W. J. Herbert
arrives at the conviction of equality between the species as
evidenced not in the rather difficult conception of doctrine
or theory but in the shared understanding of the fate of all
species, their vulnerabilities in the face of time. In "Shani-
dar, First Flower People," the elegiac confrontation with
the meaning of death in the long history of species, the poet
reflects on the death of one human species. It is a consider-
ation that comes near the end of the collection, reminding
us of how the collection begins with an epigraph that lays
out the vulnerability of all living species but also presents a
conception of equality that is predicated on the long-view
history of extinction and survival. This collection does not
seek to propose an activist view of environmental action
but, instead, seeks to lay the context of our existence in a
world of change.

The collection could be crudely described as a "threaded"
sequence in the manner of a trendy pattern in contempo-
rary nonfiction where two quite disparate and seemingly
unrelated threads of narrative are set beside each other in
a metonymic manner. In Herbert's hands, however, the
treatment of a tantalizingly elusive reflection on a relation-
ship between a child, Sarah, and herself, as a mother figure,
allows her to explore very intimate wrestlings with mortal-
ity on a domestic level (a girl coping with the news of her
mother's illness, the stages of that illness, and, ultimately, as
in the unsettling poem "After My Burial, Sarah Asks," the

poet's death). She tells the story of a counselor talking to a daughter who has just lost her mother. In these moments, Herbert's economy of language and her sense of timing is impeccable, matched only by the manner in which she is able to remind us that the entire collection is, in a sense, a meditation on mortality, from the grand scale of eons to the immediate tragedies of a mother's death:

> *Sarah*, he's saying
> with a clipped "ah" at the end of it,
>
> as if this syllable is that filament
> about to break—
>
> as if he is the one who is breaking it.

At the center of *Dear Specimen* is an ambitious and intellectual and moral conundrum—the core complex of ecological art, of the ecological poetry. Herbert quotes Richard Ryder questioning humanity's capacity to "oppress" other species. In a poem entitled "Speciesism," the poet proposes the litany of abuses done on other species. In a sense, one is being asked to enter into a metaphorical discussion that aligns racism or sexism with speciesism. Herbert is most interested in exploring the complexity of this concept, its origins and its nature, but it is clear that she is carefully pushing against the kind of thinking that positions humans as standing on top of the chain of species, and thus enabled by a series of inalienable rights to dominate and conquer. She addresses the other creatures, and thus is embarked on a proposition that they are equal to the human species. One imagines that there is much in her treatment of the subject that could give other species pause about appropriations, condescension, and contradictions, in which their "agency" does not have a genuine place in the work. Herbert appreciates the beginning of her ecological discourse as a moral continuum taking shape in her poems. The sins of humans arrive with some irony, none of which is to be mistaken for humor. The metaphor and simile are elements of species-ism that the poet seems aware of:

> dark bars and mottled
>
> browns of your
>   feathers dressed, as if
>
> we were Edwardians
>   and you, swag on a hat.

In "Squander," this metaphorical engagement with nature welcomes the dignity of the creature as a model for the human. There is no doubt a clear anthropomorphism is at work here, but in these instances, as in many of Herbert's poems, the other species is the gift-giver, the means by which the human gains her understanding of herself. Herbert declares herself to be a magpie, dazzled by and drawn to Walmart glitter. But the poem turns into a complaint about the so-called glitter that humans leave as trash, that draws the magpie in, and leads to danger for the magpie:

> I don't connect the bracelet
>   I buy at Walmart to a gold
>   mine's cyanide heap

leaching or the made-
  with-fracked-gas plastics
    that I throw in the trash

to the survivor in an as-yet
  unnamed epoch
    who'll sniff the fossil

bones of a predator
  unknown to it, though
    the skull that it licks

will likely be ours
  and, even if this creature
    resembles the rat-sized

mammal that evolved when
  dinosaurs died, by what blood
    chemistry will it breathe?

By the end of the collection, it is clear that Herbert is celebrating the natural world through poems that might easily be called odes to a menagerie of creatures. The list includes doves, hawks, terns, crows, eagles, copperhead snakes, turtles, salamanders, squids, water scorpion, white-tailed deer, waterfowl, and dovekie. She includes in this list extinct creatures that she has encountered as fossils and creatures she has found listed in biological texts and in various discourses on nature. In many instances, she addresses these creatures directly, allowing the function of the imagination to explore the ideas that occupy her in this work. In "Tipping Point," her rationale for these poems is presented in the manner of one who regards the state of the earth as an urgent concern. The creatures are talismans of significant meaning for her:

> Time's short, you say. From gorge to overlook,
> Earth's angry, now, no longer on her knees
> and, still, we decimate with each degree:
>
> black rhino, blue whale, leatherback, chinook.
> No rainbow, just a grim trajectory.
> Marvels archived in dust's dissympathy.

Her fascination with birds does teach us a great deal about how animals move her and give meaning to her. This engagement with birds is a kind of refuge, the refuge poets associate with their art—a place where meaning and beauty coexist, a place where the troubled pains of living are allowed to find expression, even when the pain persists. Often, in Herbert's collection, one discerns a delicate dance with the ars poetica—never forced, and never pretentious:

> More chemo. He withdrew, black terrapin
>
> that settled in the mud and disappeared
> while I sat there and thought about the box.
>
> That fall as days seemed slow and cold, I cleared
> out ivy, watched the "v" of passing flocks
>
> while under eaves a twig cup, half-hewn boat,
> hung on, like him, unraveling. Remote.

The intimacy of a relationship, the daunting truth of sickness and chemotherapy, the quest for some solace in nature, the wonderful fascination with what nature can do, and the helplessness in the face of the things of the world, all come together in this elegant poem.

The poems constitute an ecology of place, and an ecology of a land that is not defined by the borders and the names of places that humans have only recently marked with names. Instead, she is tracing the ecology of various species, those that have persisted in the present and even those that have left only the trace of fossils. Herbert trusts the "science" of things, the legacy of "study" that, for her, derives its meaning from its original Latin root—a reach for something livelier than the cold practice of studying: *"zeal, pursuit, eagerness, interest, devotion."* Herbert is fascinated by what she can learn, and in poems, it is enough to observe, to note, to record what she has seen of these creatures. What generates passion is that she is in dialogue with these imagined creatures. I say imagined, not because they are inventions but because her act of enlivening them, achieved through her use of direct speech to the creatures, is reflective of her passion, her deep interest in the mysteries of these creatures, and these mysteries are articulated through the enrichment of the imaginative impulse—of allowing the facility of her capacity to conceive language to capture that which she is seeing. This insistent fascination lies at the heart of the poems.

In "Hybrid," the poet speaks to the once threatened red wolf that is now recovering but doing so by crossbreeding with other species. It is clear that the poet is bothered by this, bothered by the quest to retain a kind of ecological purity, and yet she is empathetic to the wolf for crossbreed-

ing. Here, again, the human is in dialogue with the crea-
ture—imagined as conscience, so much so that the rhetori-
cal gesture that frames the poem found in these lines, "If
you're a red wolf, / you know what I'm talking about," is
somewhat hubristic and bold in its presumption. Here the
precarious ideological conundrum of anthropomorphism
is enacted. The discursive need is to articulate a radical
philosophy pushing against the ravages of "speciesism," yet
the poet can't avoid falling prey to the traps of this political
discourse.

Refreshingly, the study of these creatures becomes
translated into the study of the self, the study of the body
that must deal with human frailty and human mortality.
This study is expressed as a hope, a desire, and then as
a reality—a practice of the lyric art. It is this, then, that
grounds our emotional engagement with this work. Scat-
tered artfully throughout the collection, the poet arrives,
fully human, vulnerable, intellectually vital and present,
to remind us that she is part of this grand ecology in which
the human species is merely one among many. The inti-
macies of her life, her family, and her body, these are part
of this larger "earth" enterprise. *Dear Specimen* is a finely
wrought work of art, and a splendid introduction to a poet
of exciting promise and possibility.

KWAME DAWES
LINCOLN, NEBRASKA
JUNE 8, 2021

~ I ~

A Homo Sapiens on the Brink of Extinction Speaks to the Fossil Mosasaurus

The asking subject in every question already
has something of the object about which
he asks, otherwise he could not ask.
                                    —PAUL TILLICH

                            If you could lunge
from a cave with your whip-bait tail,
shock a sea bird with your strike

then, bit by bit, with its belly in your grip
swallow it whole,

                        why didn't you survive?
Even now, your stone-slick bones
frighten me. *Mosa*,

                lord of the late Cretaceous,
though there's nothing left of you
but these few bleached

            runes, you seem alive
                                    & I'm dying.

Yesterday,
as if a fossil had come to life

                        I watched my ribs lift,
though what appeared
on the black & white screen

seemed a skeletal
outline with no fleshy remnant,

                as if I hadn't disappeared
                                completely,

but left a signal
     so that, far into the future,

someone might puzzle over me,
     the way I'm puzzling over you.

Lyuba

As they sketch an extinct bison,
shrew, or whatever skeleton

     calls out to them,
girls in hushed voices talk about *Stranger
Things*; *Love, Simon*; *A Wrinkle in Time*.

   On white paper, the femurs
they ink are as black as the tar-soaked ones

     they study,
using pens as delicate
as their own smallest bones.

Each girl carries walnuts & Clif bars
in a paper bag & because each bag

     seems a little belly,
I think of Lyuba, baby mammoth
unearthed from the tundra,

   mother's milk inside her,
eyelashes intact, as if she's only asleep.
Isn't she graceful?

the teacher whispers
to a student who's staring

at an extinct La Brea stork.
The girl hesitates.

Dropping her eyes to the blank page
she inks the bird—

beak open, shrieking.

Speak to Me

Flail each
       of your thousand feet or,

at least, unarmor your plates
       and let me see inside you.

How does the luminescent
       blue of your body

expand then close up again,
       fluent as a geisha's tassled fan?

Spill into me, *Millipede*,
       give me your grace,

your sticky, sensuous
       legs, your luminous tube:

blue-edged and nested
       row of potters' bowls

glazed and fired and stacked;
       your anus clean and smooth.

If I turn you upside down,
       your shelled head is an embryo.

After a Miscarriage, My Daughter Asks

Why did I lose another one?

And so I reach for her,
      remembering
      how she would
warm the bruised bodies

she'd find beneath
      the sparrow's nest,
      tuck them inside her
sweater, so they could feel

the heat of her breast,
      though they
      were already dead.
She would look at me then,

as she's looking at me now,
      gaze frozen
      as if she's holding
a bowl of spilled bones

that she wants
      to put back,
      though the bowl
is filled now with blood.

Millipede

Blue rune,
your body curves
like an opalescent
necklace;

legs, a tiny legion
yoked to the oar.

Are those glossy tiles
your eyes?

No nose.
Yellow cap,
a watchman's;

the dot on each
segment
of your shell,
a pin prick

hole your spirit
slips through
as you glide over
twigs and rocks,

rippling sentence
with a hundred
periods
to punctuate.

Aerial View

I nursed a young wisteria, a vine
whose shoots each spring surged, tidelike. Plaited. Roped
around my arbor's beams, a shrewd design
to harbor doves, a leaf sea gently sloped
and eddying with shadow swells. Then no
rains came and though I watered vines, drought left
a meagre loom to hide their nest and so,
by shifting strands, I rewove weft
and warp and saved both from the hawk, I thought.
But did I see through leaves as raptors do?
What stupid hubris! Crushing ribs, he caught
her breast and she, still struggling as he flew,
flapped useless wings. That night her mate came back.
More brutal, still, that second hawk attack.

Least Tern

You seem so perfect

> though all your feathers are gone
> and you're glowing,

each bone shining through your skin,

> the jar that holds you
> just wide enough
> for your hip joints to spread

and your arms
to cock themselves by your side,

> as if you're still
> a fledgling in a nest, legs gripping
> its edge, half-open wings

unfolding, but someone's bent
your neck so that your spine's collapsed,

> and how will you fly like that?

Seamless Bead

Smooth and cool with a streak
the color of fog

broken by a coastline,
the dove's egg

because Sarah was pregnant
again,

seemed to be a gift wrapped in sticks
that fell away

and I worried
that a crow might carry away
or winds lift

this wisp
of would-be belly and bone: shucked pea,
its heart still beating.

Embryonic Daughter

A miniature female within the parent
sporophyte led to the evolution of seeds.

Late Paleozoic & here you are
before your species

     disappears & delta
ironstone makes invisible

        all but your fossil
stems shining in a shale bed,

     bee-sized leaves
        kissing them.

If I could raise
     your layered veil, time's

trial & error accretions,
        would I find you

alive?—
girl miracle, sweet

progenitrix of gingko
& spruce, avatar

     stilled by a stone wind.

Fragile Eagle

*The La Brea Tar Pits' Page Museum
displays fossils of extinct & extant species.*

Eyes, glistening hollows.
Blackened claws. Breast bone sunk
                between scrawny

haunches
as if you're squatting by a campfire,

though your tailbone's a comb
for a countess, tines shining
        with Ice Age asphalt.

And your elbows!
        Oh, Ichabod, here you are again,

pole bean behind a parlor curtain
as a fiddler sweats in his too-tight jacket
        & women in petticoats

sway in the arms of men wearing
breeches & blue stockings:
        no one's bones are showing.

Mounting the Dove Box

I ordered it online for him and then
nailed it under the eaves where he could see
a pair fly in and out with twigs, and when

chicks fledged, they'd wobble testing wings and he
would be distracted, maybe feel less pain

but no doves seemed to nest, though one flew in
and we both held our breath. Then heavy rain.
More chemo. He withdrew, black terrapin

that settled in the mud and disappeared
while I sat there and thought about the box.

That fall as days seemed slow and cold, I cleared
out ivy, watched the "v" of passing flocks

while under eaves a twig cup, half-hewn boat,
hung on, like him, unraveling. Remote.

Resin Specimen

Turtle skulls.
    You, *Snapper*, beside your

ignominious resin twin.
    He's a Mardi Gras mask,

putty skull that glistens
    with newness, catches

the light and shines
    while you're a wondrous

dull thing, bleached bone
    with holes for viscous

eyes, jaw scissored to snatch
    whatever swims by.

Who would believe your
    skull could look sinewy?

Ridges, a pale creek bed
    worn by watershed flesh,

the way a stream
    scours its own stony bed.

Dark Season

In the arbor, fungus
      spreads its melancholy
        everywhere

while shoots
      that can't find purchase
        in the air

etch themselves against it.
      Vine tangle
        like thoughts half-

dead but still connected,
      a lost philosophy.
        Or are these my griefs

trapped between vine and slat?—

the dog I didn't care for
      well enough and so
        she died, orphaned

cousin I could have loved,
      the better death
        I wanted for my father.

Dusky and Zigzag Salamanders

Thirty-five squeezed into a jar, heads
skewed, legs pressed against dusky
bellies. Range: New Brunswick

to the Carolinas. In another jar's
eerie ocean, only you, *Zigzag*,
thin as a child's pencil or clipped string;

each leg, a dwarf tree
sprouting from your underbelly. Seed eyes,
dark stars in a fingerling milky way.

The Seer

Circling and circling, I stop
to consider, not the oneness of beings,
but the coffin he's in,

how the wood must be damp,

      or maybe it's dry inside
      his vault and a mole is snuggled up
      against its buried walls,

wondering what sort of gigantic stone
flowed so far
from the river that carried it—

stone after strange-shaped stone buried in this field,

      the mole thinks as she tunnels and tunnels
      and, now, I'm tunneling with her
      and he's here, too,

but what does the skin I loved
look like after lying in such fertile,
or is it dry silence?

Nautiloid

*Of 2,500 species that evolved
in warm, shallow seas, only six survive.*

Little squid, you're swimming
as if this black granite

only seconds ago skeined you,
though you haven't siphoned

through your fleshy tube
in 400 million years.

How is it you're still glistening?—

as if reflecting the same sunlight
I felt this morning

as I walked through your sea bed.
It's a desert, now, for coyote

& scavenging rabbit, occasional
jogger with her dog, all the green-

leaved creosote
scorched stones & gravel can gather.

After My Diagnosis, Sarah Asks

They'll cure you, right?

And I remember how I'd kiss her
   and try to leave for the night,

but she'd hang on to my hand,
   tuck it under mermaid sheets,

as if she could keep it all night
   beside her and let the rest

of me go. Even then, she'd have known
   that I couldn't sever myself

to soothe her. Now her pain spikes as,
   days after a cesarean,

a pair of just-opened eyes
   locks on hers, his suckling

insistent. And so she asks, again,
   for the impossible.

Water Scorpion, Magnified 40x

To study, from the Latin studium:
zeal, pursuit, eagerness, interest, devotion.

Why scorpion? Scrawny
insect Ichabod, you're nothing

like H. arizonensis,
the Sonoran's fat Santa,

stinger gunning for spiders
and mice. I can't see

a menacing tail either, only
snorkels rising from your limb

forest, thorax pinned.
Who snatched you from

the mud where your mother
laid you among weeds above

the waterline to keep you out
of harm's way until you hatched?

Nymph. Needle bug. Water stick.

In Sarah's nightmare,
I am scooped up into the air

and carried into a lab
where a biologist, pinching

tweezers, fixes bits of me
to slides that he will study.

Waterfowl, Dovekie

Four in a drawer lie belly-
    up, curved
feet crisscrossed beneath
    short

tail feathers and you,
    smallest,
are a downy sausage. Who
    primped you

for this? Picked your lice
    and smoothed
the graying feathers
    of your neck?

And why here in the humid
    Carolinas, *little Auk*?
You, who would flock to the edges
    of pack ice

and dive, wings and feet
    swimming
furiously; your call, a loud
    hysterical laugh.

White-Tail

Yes, they will let me pet you,
    dear Deer. Sheared at the shoulders
        and placed on the table,

you look up to the Heavens
    with the same lace of black lashes
        and wide-open eyes

as mine. Though you
    have no arms to entreat with,
        no palms to open

and upturn, still your ears
    outstretch, and those ears!
        Such big dishes,

they must hear whatever
    excuse God is giving you.
        If you were mounted

on a wall, you would look
    straight out at me, asking:
        Why are we here?

~ III ~

Celestial Mechanics

       Though once
I hiked through gypsum dunes
10,000 years old,

                       what galaxies
you must have passed, *Meteorite*,
as you hurtled

from a distance irrelevant to measure
& so, too, time.

           Pocked skull with your back
hacked open, half-formed
head of the *Thinker*,

                       as if God,
like Rodin's figure lost
in thought, contemplated

               how to imbue you
with His ideas of the Universe,
           its origins.

               But after creating
Mosasaurus, predator of the late
Cretaceous,

then sculpting T. Rex
& its victims, didn't He hesitate

to forge & unleash us?

American Beaver

I love you, *Castor*,
       I can't help myself.

I don't know if it's because you gnaw
whatever you need

       then, for months,
fall into a deep almost-sleep

the way your cousin did
       through Pleistocene winters

while wooly mammoths froze
in sinkholes.

          I love your slender paws
and pudgy face, how you swim

nose up in the Hudson amid PCBs
and cadmium but *Castor*,

           it's your tail
that puts me over the top:

the way you waggle back and forth
smashing the water

to warn kits away from a bobcat,
       anchored barge leaking tar sands.

After His Nightmare, Sarah Asks

Will you tell him a bedtime story?

"Once a manatee and her calf swam
in a lagoon where herons and egrets feed . . ."

"What do they eat?" he asks.

"Manatees eat sea grass,
but the calf is so young that it suckles

its mother, and once there was a boy
who, paddling his kayak,

would watch water lap over their great
gray backs."

Seth's quiet. Before he was born,
Sarah, heavy-boned, seemed to float,

undulating
to ebbs and swells as if the moon,
too, was impatient for a baby.

Now via Skype,
I see them snuggling. Above his bed,
a dangling sun. Venus. Mars.

Earth so adrift in the dark,

Seth seems uneasy
beneath it. Does he imagine fevered
        soil, poisoned sea grass?

                Mom, finish the story!

"I don't know how it ends, Sarah,"
        I say, "but the boy loves

the manatees' whiskered faces,
flippers tipped with fingernails,
                        like his,

and he wonders if the calf
        feels as drowsy as he does,

                and where
the tide's cradle will carry them."

Fledgling

Migrating pole to pole in search of a second summer,
terns annually fly up to 50,000 miles.
— ARCTIC TERN MIGRATION PROJECT

If halfway to the Weddell Sea, he drops
into the North Atlantic, it's because

he found too little krill to eat. Still, does
this mean he took off far too soon? What stops

a chick from starving, if he flies? Have lots
of terns learned how to heed the risky buzz

a novice chick (who still has downy fuzz)
can't know warns winds are over 30 knots?

The problem is: it's not just this one bird
who can't find food when warming seas thin krill,

or when late winds delay a coastal spike
in plankton—it's the auklet, puffin, murre,

once breast-fed blue whale calf who tries to fill
her baleens' fringe, her low-pitched moans ghostlike.

Speciesism

1. Viper

Stopped smiling. Tongue
    stilled. Every scale
        that slid through cypress
    and dry pine
heavy now with formaldehyde,

your creamy underbelly's
    swelled with it
        and, though, head thrust up,
    you once
surged across the salt marsh

to sun in pignut hickory,
    someone's
        cracked your spine to coil
    and jimmy you
into this jar.

2. *Endangered Aye Aye*

Who took your body to the lab
     and brought your skeleton back?—

forepaws and rear feet
     mounted in a straight line along

a tree limb bought from
     Burlington Biological Supply.

You would never have perched
     like that and, even if

you still wanted to scramble
     head first from the canopy,

there's only the bony
     ghost of the hand you once used

for grasping, no way to tap
     on tree bark, rip it open,

and reach in with your crazy-long middle digit
     to pull out the sweet, larval meat.

3. *Great Horned Owl*

They say the mouse at dusk
    can't see your shadow

or hear your noiseless flight;
    that you puncture her

stomach, hide her carcass
    and keep hunting,

later thaw her to tear out
    the tenderest parts

but here you are—
    dark bars and mottled

browns of your
    feathers dressed, as if

we were Edwardians
    and you, swag on a hat.

Squander

I'm still a magpie. If it glitters,
      I want it, no matter
            the cost—

I don't connect the bracelet
      I buy at Walmart to a gold
            mine's cyanide heap

leaching or the made-
      with-fracked-gas plastics
            that I throw in the trash

to the survivor in an as-yet
      unnamed epoch
            who'll sniff the fossil

bones of a predator
      unknown to it, though
            the skull that it licks

will likely be ours
      and, even if this creature
            resembles the rat-sized

mammal that evolved when
      dinosaurs died, by what blood
            chemistry will it breathe?

Tipping Point

If you choose to fail us, I say we will never forgive you.
— GRETA THUNBERG,
U.N. CLIMATE ACTION SUMMIT, SEPT. 2019

Fierce heat waves, wildfires, climate refugees,
acidic coral, glacial melt, and look—

a marmoset, orb weaver's filigree,
an algae-coated sloth whose canopy's
on fire, though she gave birth last night. Her nook

inside a lush Brazilian tree
which once sequestered carbon, helped us breathe,

is burning. We've done little to unhook
Earth from this carbon juggernaut, the greed
of fossil fuel producers, energy

that's not renewable, and so you took
your protest to the streets of Karachi,

Cape Town, New York, Bangkok, Berlin, Sydney.

Time's short, you say. From gorge to overlook,
Earth's angry, now, no longer on her knees
and, still, we decimate with each degree:

black rhino, blue whale, leatherback, chinook.
No rainbow, just a grim trajectory.
Marvels archived in dust's dissympathy.

Errant Eagle

Extinct species extracted from the La Brea Tar Pits.

You might have died
        trying to pluck
        a shrew from
the pit, but you couldn't lift it,

both of you held fast
        in asphalt
        near a woolly
mammoth wailing

to escape. In the museum
        as Sarah struggles
        to haul up
a footed stem whose end

is trapped in a bucket
        of the goo
        that held you,
we hear your screech—

mad beat of your one
        free wing,
        but the bucket's
redundant. No need

to pretend how
        you'd have sensed
        the inevitable
now that we're trapped,

too. Though unlike us,
        you were
        never to blame
for the pit, its making.

Put Bones in Pit When Finished

The Zuhl Museum's Kids Corner features paintings
of extinct marine species, sand box & plastic fossils.

Coloring book. Puzzle. Pieces
of T. Rex to bury; pretend eons flash by
      as femur, spine, ribs fossilize.

      Mural of larger-than-life
trilobites: eyes berry red & big as a fist;
        ridged shells

round as a star ship, nautiloids floating
beside them. At a table, a woman
                mulls over fossil

fuel stocks her broker thinks will blossom,
while a child probes for pieces of T. Rex
        & the Barbie she buried.

If Oil Rigs Raise You Like Lazarus from the Shale of the Permian Basin

Jesus said: Whosoever liveth
and believeth in me shall never die.
—JOHN 11:26

I can see your eyes, *Trilobite*,
& I want to touch them.

        Ridges rippling
across your broad black shell,
arms waving,

     or are those legs
churning toward the reef

        of a Paleozoic sea
that I will never see?

If I could travel back in time,
      I would lay my body

down beside you,
gills heaving as the ocean's

carbon dioxide rises,
      & I would apologize,

confess: If we raise you,
        no one can save us.

~ IV ~

Abnormal Echo

Though magnified
    and enhanced,
        these sounds
    aren't prerecorded
or amplified,

the heart here
    is alive
        and it's mine:
    a technician's
wand pressing

against my ribcage
    to measure
        the slow leap
    of each leaf
as it struggles

to stop a clot
    smaller
        than the eye
    of a recluse spider
from flying off

to settle
in my brain's
mud threads
and webs, spongy
wings from which

these words form,
remnant pulse
of the specimen
a biologist lays
on her table.

Before the Bonfire

I haven't swept it for a week, though leaves
like a light rain drop every day
until the side yard below the sparrow's nest
wears silk, a sari shimmering on the hips
of a girl asleep on winter's doorstep.
Still, I don't sweep. Meds and tests
have made me moody, ruthless. And I want
to watch her silk turn brittle before it burns.

Bridge Constructs in Modern Technology

Formerly used only as a bridging device, implanted
pumps may now prolong life for heart failure
patients ineligible for a transplant.

If a boy's Chevy didn't
        slide through
                a yellow light
        and, so, wasn't
pulverized by a bridge

that collapsed
        days after installation,
                concrete ribbon
        dangling above a sump
of rubble and dust—

If a girl stayed up late
        watching *Survivor*,
                Ghost Island and, so,
        wasn't crossing six lanes
of the Tamiami Trail

beneath what was dubbed
        the "instant" bridge,
                though it wasn't finished
        and she'd have been
looking up at it—

If a worker called in sick
        as the ribbon snapped,
                though six others
        weren't so lucky
and the accident

wasn't an *accident*,
        engineers aware
                of the danger
        before others
escaped it, then

what are the odds
        that I could slip
                through the sieve?—

Cardinal, You Would Not Believe

How you sing
as I lay you on the interactive table,

red belly brilliant,
though someone's collapsed

your feathered crest,
and your tail is tied with white string,

and your bed's a foam strip
to which you've been pinned.

But listen!—
If I press this button, katydids

scrub their socks
in a washboard thicket, while a cricket

gambler rattles
mesquite, handful of lucky dice.

Hybrid

Once extinct in the wild, reintroduced red
wolves look like a distinct species, but their
genetics show mixing with other canids.
— U.S. FISH AND WILDLIFE

If you're a red wolf,
you know what I'm talking about.

You're almost gone.

Why wouldn't you mate
with gray wolves, coyotes, dogs?

I'd do it, give up the coral edges
of my ears, my reddish brows,

even the tawny fur
that blossoms down my snout
and slips into my whiskers.

But, *Red*, don't change your nose,

heady well that every scent
falls into: rotting cypress, lynx pee
wet in leaf fall;

the tree frog's throat
rattling like little nails riveting

into your skin, milk snake
shushing pine needles as you pass.

A Pastoral Topography

Above his bed, he'd hung a lithograph
of clouds,

    or was it icebergs?——

                snow geese
floating off a coast, cotton
in a Sea Island field.

    He'd imagined lambs

in the Eden above us
blessing what was left of his life

and wanted to touch each one
but I'd said:

    Stop pretending.

In the end, he'd pointed,
Keep this picture, so I hung it

on my stairway wall. If I tilt
my head, ovals float

    in a heaven of ice

or air that lightens
as I climb, as if breezes rising

      to the airborne plain

of another place
are lifting me with them and, soon,

I'll become as light

as he did that day,
between the time I closed my eyes

to escape his labored breathing,
and the moment after.

Riddles of Flock & Bone

Not because of your feathers:
        yours, *Merganser*, are streaked
                to hide you beneath

willow leaves over-
        hanging a stream, while his
                are a frantic Fat Tuesday,

blues paisleying
        all over the place.

And not because of your beaks,
        one curved for cracking seeds;
                the other, black tongs

for brackish water. Courting
        dance, then? But how regal
                your tail's sweep, *Pheasant*,

and how comic your cousin's
        short fan of head feathers:
                black-edged goth

with webbed, unfortunate
        feet. You're not even the same

species, family, or order,
    though you're both *chordata*:
        vertebrates and *aves*: birds.

So is it this?
    Your wings' downy underside,
        lilt of ribs to ease your breathing.

Homo Sapiens

Past the mammoth
head of a moose,
pine stump with squirrel
in mid-descent,

and raccoon
whose ringed tail points
to life outside

this window,
which seems only for a moment
to hold you all

here, in this dark room—

there's a human skeleton
hanging from the hook
of a rolling stand:

a man only
a little taller than I am.

In the End, Sarah Asks

Do you remember Spirit Rock?

And I picture us
meditating as a blue
             broom gathers

itself out over the ocean
        to sweep across hilltops,

the summer
coming to scorch us,
        not even on the horizon yet—

still days of scattering
rain before it would all
           come apart.

We could sit again, now, she says,
but I imagine her

       standing
in the Trader Joe's check-out line,

eyes red, skin puffy underneath.
        Sarah, I say. *You . . .*

but she interrupts: *Mom,*
        don't worry about me.

She brings tea, rakes leaves,
        face beaming with heat.

Shanidar, First Flower People

In the mid-fifties, a cluster of fossils
of an extinct human species was found
in a cave in northern Iraq.

I don't know which
I like least: the idea
of being cremated
using fossil
fuels that pollute,
or the mental
image of my body
being burned—

how could it not hurt?

So composted
with wood chips
& alfalfa,
skin blistered
then grayed,
then greened?

No, lay me down
in that cave where
others were covered
with cornflower,

hyacinth, yarrow
& hollyhock.
Leave me

unsheathed,
so that time
swaddles me in
muddy vestments,
every bone
turned to stone
with a mineral's kiss.

~ V ~

The Smell of Almost Rain

High up, a rusted hoop's
    dangling
        from a cracked backboard,
    ragged net
missing whiskers,

while from beneath
    a warped porch,
        a mutt with swollen feet
    and balding muzzle
is wobbling toward me

and farther south,
    an ice shelf's shearing
        away from its glacier,
    bears stranded,
no sea ice to hunt from,

while here there's
    despair over
        the state of the nation,
    its captain obsessing
like Ahab—

but, for now,
        none of these
                is bothering me
        because I'm high
on a med that slakes

pain, and the drug's rioted,
        stunned, and distilled
                this day into a large-
        hearted leaf with
a bug crawling up it,

fist of raspberries
  budding nearby while
    Sarah's cattle dog dives
  into a leaf lake
at the edge of the Rite Aid lot,

green spears spilling
  over him, as if he's
    being guillotined
  by spring's manic,
weedy happiness.

Sea Lily

Related to starfish & sea urchin, crinoids
flourished before the Permian Extinction.

Once in West Texas, I searched for you
on a fossil reef whose rim was neither
   buried deep beneath Fort Stockton,

nor pitched too high
in the Guadalupe Mountains for me to reach,
    though I still had to hunt

for you on the jagged limestone's
underside, get down on my hands & knees
    to see you: thimble-sized

& without the lithe stem that once
rooted you to the reef. But, later,
   in the museum where I found you

again, in a fossil piece of sea floor,
you seemed to float as if still feeding
    on plankton gliding by.

Lily, why do we have so little time?

At the Museum of Permian Extinctions

*Pliny the Elder called fossils of spiral-shelled ammonites
"horns of Ammon," after depictions of an Egyptian god.*

When will we be what you are? Dissolved by the ocean's unraveling.

Triage

A woman stumbles
      into the ER.
         The receptionist is calm,
the room cool. Outside,

it's dinnertime
      as the hospital's
      body moves
like a whale that, breathing,

leaves wind and light
      behind it as it dives.
      Inside its belly,
a cavernous room

where the woman's
      in a bed now,
      her heart,
a dinghy bobbing

wildly as the night
      sea deepens,
      fills with the frail
whose faces collapse, as if

pressed by the weight
      of water and their sons
      and daughters
can do nothing to lift it

from them, can't feel
      the temperature
      drop and the pressure
rise around the woman

who sinks quietly and soon,
        she's so deep
        that, to capture
what light is left in the darkness

around her, her eyes
        leave her body and grow out on long stalks
        and when she hits
bottom, the bump jars

her heart, but her arms glow
        as if lit by a strange
        fish whose forehead
gleams as it glides by

and the woman dreams of harp
        sponge, sea whip
        coral, the luminous
arms of light-tipped squid.

American Copperhead

Holding your shed skin,
    a boy looks you up on the touchscreen.
                Around him, specimens

of snowy owl, Canada goose,
    cougar with one leg descending
                from a rock ledge,

track lights, slide screen, speaker,
    carpet patterned like a forest floor.
                In the hallway, an elevator

dings and a couple with a child
steps out. Through floor-to-ceiling windows,
                they see woodrats

sealed in a display case,
    labeled drawers, hand-held globe,
                microscope which the child

is lifted up to look through.
    At dusk, a biologist gathers up carapace,
                jawbone, shed skin, pelt.

Viper, do you see the bare trees
    beyond this building, hear the siren
        in the street?—

A motorcycle at the head of a somber
    convoy is ferrying someone across the city
        to the river's edge.

After My Burial, Sarah Asks

herself . . .
well, nothing, really. It's me
she wants to talk to but she doesn't know how,

and I can't help her. *Sarah,*

a counselor is saying, now that my daughter's
finally opened a brochure

which lists follow-up services
hospice provides. *Sarah* . . .
this stranger is saying,

not gently, or slowly, or softly
the way I would have,

and now I'm picturing the brittle
filament that runs from his landline
to the receiver she's holding:

Sarah, he's saying
with a clipped "ah" at the end of it,

as if this syllable is that filament
about to break—

as if he is the one who is breaking it.

Dear Specimen

You, whose tail's pinned to foam strip
or whose underbelly's heavy

       with formaldehyde,
who's squeezed into a jar or shell slit;
and you,

who lie belly-up in a shut drawer
or sheared at the shoulders and displayed

on a table or whose neck
is bent so that we can see you better—

you haven't answered my questions
and now I'm here, preserved

       and catalogued
while Sarah stands over my stone
and she's forgotten

her tissues again
and is using her sleeve, which is soaking

     wet, and she glances at the pit-
digging machine and mounded dirt,
then up

                  at the ducks
and wonders what kind they are.
Back home,

she'll search the internet
and discover that they are you, *Merganser*,

            flying south again for the winter.

Day Shift/Night Shift

Of our genus, estimated to be 1.5–2.5 million years old,
only one species remains: Homo sapiens (wise man),
who emerged roughly 300,000 years ago.

1.

With her instep, Anna scoots dirty towels into the hallway outside
    room 22 of the Best Western Tucson Airport Hotel. She
    empties wastebaskets, replaces coffee packets, texts her
    daughter to say she'll be late.

2.

Rayna leans over a hotel layout, pointing to breakfast area, pool,
    fitness room & laundry. In a lull between arrivals, she
    flips off her shoe & rubs between toes where the itch is.

3.

At dusk, coyote pups denned beneath mesquite wake, mewling.
    Their mother trots across the wash to the edges of a runway
    where she'll catch mice for pups too young to hunt.

4.

At Our Lady of the Desert, Abraham rakes hackberry branches
    that have blown against gravestones, wipes his forehead
    with a bandana as creosote staves off waning rays.

5.

After midnight, the airport shuttle stops running. Lobby empty,
    the hotel clerk nods off, the desert supine & soundless

6.

while in the Santa Catalinas thirty miles above coyote pups,
    creosote, and the hotel's slumbering bones, Oracle
    granite born 1440 million years ago still moves.

At the Sea Floor Exploration Exhibit, Sarah Asks

Ghost fish, tail flapping
like a translucent scrap
of linen in the wind,
flag of surrender
with a spine inside,
eyes riding on slow
light through the deep
ocean's darkness:

Do you know what my mother was looking for?—

Why she came to you
with questions
though you are here
only in photos
and, as it failed,
her heart worked hard
and, so, she was always tired.

Did she imagine what you might know

of the dark zones?—
trenches erased by time
as sediments drift to the sea

floor, carrying the dead
who fall to feed you:

you whose nights
and days are spent near vents
that release the heat
of what lies deeper,

please, tell me what you told her.

Epilogue: To a Trilobite

After oil rigs raised you from the basin,
          and we burned you
      until we passed

              the tipping point—

blue whales starving for krill
            stopped calving,
      manatees ate poisoned
         sea grass, polar bears

            sank in open sea.

Cities flooded. Crops failed.
Those who could, headed north
        to the Arctic Circle

      to fish cisco in Great Bear Lake,
though even that fresh water
          relic was long ago

tainted by radium
      mined for the Manhattan Project.

Still, no one stopped us
          from swarming onto sacred land
                    with its legend

of a magic caribou boy who,
          enchanted by a moonlit herd,

                    no longer wanted to be human.

ACKNOWLEDGMENTS

Many thanks to the editors and staff of the following publications in which versions of these poems first appeared, sometimes with different titles.

Alaska Quarterly Review:
"A Pastoral Topography"
"Hybrid"

The Atlantic:
"Squander"

Boulevard:
"Aye Aye"
"Before the Bonfire"
"Lyuba"
"A Homo Sapiens on the Brink of Extinction
    Speaks to the Fossil Mosasaurus"

Crab Orchard Review:
"Speak to Me"
"Waterfowl, Dovekie"
"Least Tern"
"American Beaver"
"Resin Specimen"
"White-Tail"

Hampden-Sydney Review:
"Abnormal Echo"

Nimrod:
"The Smell of Almost Rain"
"Cardinal, You Would Not Believe"

Pleiades:
"Aerial View"
"Errant Eagle"

River Styx:
"Great Horned Owl"
"Viper"
"Water Scorpion, Magnified 40x"
"Dusky and Zigzag Salamanders"
"Homo Sapiens"

Salamander:
"Seamless Bead"

The Southwest Review:
"Mounting the Dove Box"

"Mounting the Dove Box" also appeared in *Best American Poetry 2017*, Natasha Trethewey and David Lehman (eds.), Simon and Schuster, New York, 2017.

"Dark Season" appeared in *Beyond the Lyric Moment*, Natal, Sandstrom, Thompson (eds.), Tebot Bach, Huntington Beach, CA, 2014.

My gratitude to Kwame Dawes, who selected *Dear Specimen* from among many worthy manuscripts. His faith in the importance of the work means the world to me. A special thanks also to B. H. Fairchild, mentor and first believer; Maurya Simon, Barbara Schwartz, and Meghan

Dunn, for their meticulous attention to the manuscript; and Tim Carrier, whose insight made the completion of this work possible.

Thanks to my Claremont Writers' Group: Fran McConnel, Cindy Tuell, Nancy Ware, and Maurya Simon for their years of generous critique and companionship. For expertise and encouragement, thanks to Kathleen Ossip, her 92nd St. Y manuscript workshop, and poet Dan Kraines. Special gratitude to Andrew Pezzullo, whose insight and imagination were invaluable.

I am grateful to Vivian Dorsal and Fran Richey of *upstreet* for support to attend the Vermont College Post-Graduate Writers Conference. Kudos also to poets Joshua Mehigan and Jessica Greenbaum for their workshops under the auspices of Brooklyn Poets, directed by Jason Koo.

Thanks to the Arizona Poetry Center staff: Tyler Meier, Sarah Kortemeier, Julie Swarstad Johnson, Diana Delgado, and Leela Denver, all of whom provided me with a home away from home amid the center's extensive collections. Thanks also to the North Carolina Museum of Natural Sciences Discovery Room, the Page Museum at the La Brea Tar Pits, and the Zuhl Museum at New Mexico State University. Appreciation to Gibson Fay-Leblanc and Hanna Perry at the Maine Publishers and Writers Alliance for their tireless advocacy and, especially, to Arisa White for her insightful workshop.

Unending thanks to Daniel Halpern, Beth Dial, and the dedicated folks at the National Poetry Series, and to Helene Atwan and her marvelous team at Beacon Press.

As always, gratitude for the love and support of my family: Peter, Rachel, Sophie, Andrew, Lee, and Oz.

W. J. Herbert's work was awarded the Anna Davidson Prize and was selected by Natasha Trethewey for inclusion in *Best American Poetry 2017*. Her poetry, fiction, and reviews have appeared in *Alaska Quarterly Review*, the *Antioch Review*, *Boulevard*, *New Ohio Review*, *Pleiades*, *Southwest Review*, and elsewhere. Born in Cleveland, Ohio, she was raised in Southern California, where she earned a bachelor's in studio art and a master's in flute performance. She lives in Kingston, New York, and Portland, Maine.

Kwame Dawes is a Ghanaian poet, actor, editor, critic, musician, and the former Louis Frye Scudder Professor of Liberal Arts at the University of South Carolina. He is now professor of English at the University of Nebraska–Lincoln and editor in chief at *Prairie Schooner* magazine.